MEN ARE FROM
I'M FROM TOTTENHAM

MEN ARE FROM MARS...
I'M FROM TOTTENHAM

Welcome to
TOTTENHAM
SPURS ARE ON THEIR WAY TO WEMBLEY.
TOTTENHAMS GOING TO DO IT AGAIN.

By Roger McCartney

MEN ARE FROM MARS
I'M FROM TOTTENHAM

Copyright

ISBN 9781973520955

BY ROGER MCCARTNEY 2

INTRODUCTION

Maybe it's because you're from Tottenham, that you love the Spurs. And maybe it's because you support the Spurs, that you will love this book too.

The name 'Tottenham' comes from a farmer called Tota whose hamlet next to the River Lea gave the name to the worldwide phenomenon that is Spurs.

The Male Psyche is like that too. An uncomplicated façade can preside over something much more complex. Here, in this book, we attempt to decode the Spurs FC mind-set and provide an insight into the secret thoughts of any male Tottenham Hotspurs fan. Tired of Spurs? You are tired of life, my son. But you will never tire of this book; for it is a right old celebration of all things from the Lane: the people, the culture and the language.

BY ROGER MCCARTNEY 3

MEN ARE FROM MARS
I'M FROM TOTTENHAM

Spurs women, prepare to be enlightened. Spurs men prepare to be compromised!

BY ROGER MCCARTNEY 4

MEN ARE FROM MARS
I'M FROM TOTTENHAM

Contents

BY ROGER MCCARTNEY 5

MEN ARE FROM MARS
I'M FROM TOTTENHAM

MEN ARE FROM MARS
I'M FROM TOTTENHAM

BY ROGER MCCARTNEY 7

Secret #1: Tottenham-Born Man is The King...of Procrastination

I'm not going to mug you off, but here at the Lane, procrastination is a concept already all too familiar. We'll win the Champions League next season, thank you very much!

Admittedly, we are overdue a trophy, but Poch has got us going in the right direction, and that's the way we like it.

It was when I was strolling down Tottenham High Road the other day, anticipating another white and navy-blue victory, that it suddenly hit me. And I don't mean it was the lamppost outside the *Bill Nick* that clumped me. **It was the fact** that all my life, I have been hampered by procrastination. And I'm going to tell you exactly why that is, some other time.

BY ROGER MCCARTNEY 8

MEN ARE FROM MARS
I'M FROM TOTTENHAM

Indeed, whilst assembling this celebration of the Spurs male mind-set, I am putting off several other things that I should have already done by now. And Spurs are too, putting a few things off, like the acquisition of points, because we should be a lot higher up the Prem than we presently are. Like on top of it, for example!

Here at the Lane, we have a saying: "we'll get the three points *next week*". I don't know where this saying came from. Probably from ancient times. Gary Lineker perhaps. He's ancient.

Never mind Tottenham's motto: 'To dare is to do'. My own motto is 'Never dare to do anything today that you can put off until tomorrow' and that suits *me* just fine, thanks.

Spurs women are adept at doing several tasks at once. This is called **multitasking**. I read about that in the *Evening Standard*. Spurs geezers, however, are equally as adept at *putting off* several tasks at once. This is known as '**multi-**

thinking-about-but-not-actually-doing-any-**tasking**.'

We will routinely postpone everything until the middle of next week and then postpone it further if there is a midweek match. Me **laundry** will be done only when I spot my white and navy-blue *Dicky Dirts* making their own way over to the washing machine. **Bills** will only get paid when the bailiff personally presents them into me *German*.

And the *jam jar* will only be washed once people are starting to write childish messages, with their fingers in the dirt - such as 'up the Spurs' and that old chestnut, 'I wish my *Trouble* was as dirty as this'. Ok, admittedly, I write the some of the messages on the car myself, sometimes!

Health is the easiest issue to procrastinate over in Islington. You know when you get an appointment at the North Middlesex: that suits me! I'm right head in the sand, me, *mutton* to

BY ROGER MCCARTNEY 10

any news of a medical nature. Ruins the day, I find. I much prefer to schedule an endoscopy for the Close Season or at worst, an international break.

Blimey, if the problem is anything to do with 'downstairs', then you can forget it altogether. Funny that: fellas that support Spurs love to wave their genitals about on a boozy night down the West-end but ask them for a medical examination of said genitals and they disappear for longer than Diego Costa.

Our *Richards*, on the other hand, love a visit to the local quacks. The fact that the male locums look like George Clooney may have something to do with their real motivation to visit with such regularity, nah wot I mean. My Missus will make an appointment just to discuss colour co-ordination schemes in the lounge, or to announce a new apple crumble recipe she is planning.

BY ROGER MCCARTNEY 11

MEN ARE FROM MARS
I'M FROM TOTTENHAM

The reason for Spurs male procrastination is simple: We are primarily hunter/gatherers. We like to gather in the three points at places like Arsenal, Chelsea and West Ham, and in-between hunting and gathering expeditions, we like to maximise our downtime. Cave-geezers used to loaf about the cave; Modern-day geezers like to loaf about in front of Ben and Kammy, on *Goals On Sunday*.

After a hard day's hunting and gathering, we like to come home on the number 149 bus, to our caves, and be nurtured by our favourite Spurs cave-bird. It's been that way since old Muvver Wren's boy, Cristopher, was a lad, and St Paul's was just a glint in his eye. New age Spurs man? I'm only just catching up with pre-Bill Nicholson-Spurs Man.

One or two things have changed in the last two million years though here in Haringey. Tottenham don't just aspire to play at Wembley, now we play there every week, and we've got the

BY ROGER MCCARTNEY 12

MEN ARE FROM MARS
I'M FROM TOTTENHAM

M25 to park on. Women work, we have got a decent side again, and men will occasionally have a *Butcher's* at the babies. Can you imagine a stay-at-home cave-husband back in the ancient Old Smoke, looking after the nippers, while the *Trouble* went out and slaughtered a mammoth? It Didn't happen.

Spurs Man should not be castigated for his procrastinating nature though. It takes stern resolution and serious prioritisation skills - for us to balance a busy life at home and work and pub - and still be able to fit in eight hours watching Sky Sports.

Gawd willing and more importantly, partner willing, there will still be five minutes left at the end of the day, after *Match of the Day* of course, in which to get cosy with her-indoors. That is one appointment we do not wish to defer to a later date!

BY ROGER MCCARTNEY 13

MEN ARE FROM MARS
I'M FROM TOTTENHAM

That is, if your partner hasn't sulked off to Finsbury Park for the day, because you procrastinate so much. Or maybe she's a procrastinator too and keeps *putting off* sulking off to Finsbury Park until another day. A Richard of mine used to say; "You'll never amount to anything, me ol China, because you procrastinate too much." **I used to say, "Shut it love, let's just wait and see!**

<u>Secret #2:</u> Are You Having a *Turkish?* It's a Load of *Jackson Pollocks* That Spurs Men Think About Sex Every Six Sec...

Anyone that has done "The Knowledge" will know North London like the back of their hand. And anyone that has done 'the knowledge' of women will know that they too are self-appointed experts. On men.

But sometimes they get it *Pete Tong*. For example, there is a myth passed around the N17 area, almost entirely by that panel of experts out there, who, we shall for the purposes of this discussion, label 'Spurs women'. These 'experts' think that another body of people – whom we

shall call 'Spurs men' – think about sex with about the regularity of every six seconds.

What a load of *Jackson Pollocks*. Just as it's a load of *Jackson Pollocks* that the streets of Spurs are all covered in gold. I wish it were true.

The 'six-second rule' is an oft-quoted falsehood about the male of the Spurs species. The six-second premise was first put forward by someone, probably a female, a very long time ago, in order to explain why us men have the morality code of the lesser-spotted porcupine.

There are many myths about Spurs men, such as 'Spurs men are naturally gifted at DIY.' This statement is, of course, a load of old *pony* too.

There are other Dick-Whittington-like half-truths perpetuated about Spurs men, for example, that they all are obsessed with football. They are not: some men are obsessed

BY ROGER MCCARTNEY 16

with rugby. Another myth is that all men *rabbit* on about when they get with other men is football. They don't: they *rabbit* on about women...that talk about football. Although admittedly in between breaks from *rabbiting* on about football. And rugby.

And we all know something else that is not true: that women have got more *rabbit* than Sainsbury. What a falsehood that is. I've always thought that to be the biggest *porkie* of the lot. Sainsburys don't do rabbit.

Of course, the idea that a THFC man thinks naughty thoughts twice during the time it takes Christian Eriksen to take a corner is, quite frankly, absurd. Are you having a *bubble*? Do you not know anything about men, gel?

It's a lot more frequent than that.

Yes, the male of the species is much dirtier than the female. We all know that. Sexual thoughts

BY ROGER MCCARTNEY 17

MEN ARE FROM MARS
I'M FROM TOTTENHAM

are omnipresent. Why? Let me mansplain it for you. Because we are men. That is what we do. Naughty thoughts are what we bring to the table. For men, thoughts about sex are like number 43 buses: you don't get one down the Holloway Road for ages and then two come along at once.

Our brains work like call centres, "The next bawdy thought will be arriving in your mind in a few seconds. Please hold – your continued interest is important to us". Lewd images are certainly more reliable at arriving on time than trains on the Piccadilly line.

Of course, we think about women every six seconds. Of course, flipping of course! Why wouldn't we? But don't be too down on us, for we also think about next week's match every four seconds as well. In the time it used to take Usain Bolt to run the 100 metres, we have thought about sex twice and we have pondered next week's tricky away trip to Huddersfield.

 BY ROGER MCCARTNEY 18

MEN ARE FROM MARS
I'M FROM TOTTENHAM

But don't give us any agg about it, for we know not what we do. We cannot help it. We're men. Let she who is without sin throw the first stone.

Ouch leave it out! Watch where you are throwing those stones, will you love! Turn it in gel! Shut it!

BY ROGER MCCARTNEY 19

<u>Secret #3</u>: I Don't Do Spurs. I Am Spurs. And I Don't Do Platonic Either.

Spurs are on their way to Wembley. Every other week in fact. It's weird. And I'll tell you another thing that is weird. I had a woman as a friend once. I know, weird as you like!

We used to work together and meet up the *Billy Nick*, the spiritual drinking-home of Spurs fans. Spurs used to use it as a changing room at one time. We used to meet there on match days for a bite to eat. She was from Clapham, and although I never thought it would happen with the girl from Clapham, I went along anyway. Our common ground was a mutual interest in getting ever so slightly *elephants* before the match, and then cheering on the mighty Spurs in the Paxton Road end.

And I so wanted to sleep with her.

BY ROGER MCCARTNEY 20

MEN ARE FROM MARS
I'M FROM TOTTENHAM

Which brings me to the Deal or No Deal question and I'm ready to be asked it. Can a Spurs guy have a friendship with a Spurs sort, without wanting to sleep with her?

The short answer is no. The longer answer may lead me to further compromise the Spurs brotherhood, by revealing yet more official man-secrets.

So, buckle up, and enjoy the ride! It's going to be better than the London Eye, this is!

Anyone, who knows the North London masculine mind-set – in other words, Spurs men - will tell you that we *don't do* platonic. We would like to but we can't. We haven't got it in us. End of story. There. We can all go home now. **Black Cab for McCartney.**

What we do have in us is a massive amount of raging testosterone and a burning desire to finish above Arsenal. Oh, and did I mention a

BY ROGER MCCARTNEY 21

MEN ARE FROM MARS
I'M FROM TOTTENHAM

primeval desire to mate with every female this side of Watford. Even those from Barnet.

Admittedly, the passing of time and the advent of kebab-induced obesity have tempered this prehistoric urge, but it is still in the mix somewhere. We keep it hidden, but in our minds, everyone is being assessed as a potential sleeping partner. We can't help this thought process.

There are no female friends, just lovers waiting to happen. Men, if they're truthful, will agree with this philosophy. If they *don't* admit to it, they may tend to haemorrhage credibility.

Spurs women unwittingly put themselves in the frontline, by liking us 'as a friend'. Expect the male side of the partnership to be looking to upgrade his 'friend' status, as soon as possible. Friendships with the opposite sex are love affairs in the early stages. Hopefully.

BY ROGER MCCARTNEY 22

MEN ARE FROM MARS
I'M FROM TOTTENHAM

Back to the *Bill Nick* ladette: She never knew of my aspirations to date her, and I certainly never let on, as her boyfriend was a thoroughly nice six-foot ten rugby player from the Northumberland Road. She was fascinated with me for my ability to consume three lunchtime pints, and I was fascinated by her - for her very existence. I used to have a *Butcher's* at her lovely hazel eyes, and lust after her ruby lips as she chomped on her jellied eels. She had lovely pearly white *Hampsteads* too. She, in return, used to look longingly at me - for another white wine spritzer.

She used to bring her friend along sometimes, and I used to fancy her as well. In fact, come to think of it, I've fancied everyone that came along. I've had many female friends and I've wanted to sleep with all of them. Sometimes, male ego being what it is, I'll think I've met *The One* if a woman lets me out on the North Circular.

BY ROGER MCCARTNEY 23

MEN ARE FROM MARS
I'M FROM TOTTENHAM

Female companions are *always* better than same-sex ones, because the possibility exists of sleeping with them. With a fellow man, you just don't have that option. No, it's all about bonding over pints; and conversation that alternates between Pochettino's ability as a manager and Beyoncé's bottom.

All very riveting, but it doesn't pay the bills. And it certainly doesn't satisfy the inherent latent primeval cravings that claw at our internal beings every minute of every day. **Give me a *butcher's* at Miss Ruby Lips, in the *Billy Nick*, with her jellied eels prop, any day of the week!**

<u>Secret #4:</u> What Spurs Fellas Really Think About Rotund Lea-side Women.

Tottenham, Tottenham, no-one can stop them...but it was while I was singing this song the other day that I was suddenly besieged by Spurs-based females demanding to know what Tottenham men *really* think of their partners, being a touch on the rotund side. Well, one woman from the Blackstock Road politely asked, so here goes.

Of course, I could give you a truthful account but as it goes against the man-code to reveal our secrets; if I told you, then I would have to kill you. However, in the interests of the book, here is the absolute *Babe Ruth*, even if my instincts are to tell *porkies* and scratch my genitals.

BY ROGER MCCARTNEY 25

MEN ARE FROM MARS
I'M FROM TOTTENHAM

To get a quiet life, with the minimum amount of agg like, Spurs men have developed a knee-jerk reaction under questioning about weight issues. If we value having a full set of testicles – which we do – and to prevent our women kicking off, we will automatically respond in the negative when asked questions such as "does my bum look big in this?" Answer anything other than negative when asked this and there's going to be hell on earth; the ravens will leave the tower and there will be Armageddon up the Hornsey Road.

Here's the rub though. I am **not** telling *porkies*. **I am telling the truth**. If I thought my woman was not fanciable, I wouldn't fancy her. Ergo, I wouldn't be with her. Or, more importantly, I wouldn't have got with her in the first place. What more conclusive proof do you need of my sincerity during ~~interrogation~~ questioning?

Sure, we would all like to have girlfriends that look like Kim Kardashian. That is a given. In fact, we would all like to have for a girlfriend, Kim

BY ROGER MCCARTNEY 26

Kardashian, but this is just not possible. Just as Santa cannot get around every house in Spurs, neither can Kim.

Besides, this is Real World, UK, and just as us Spurs men don't look like Petr Cech - the ones that do are keepers, aren't they? – Spurs women don't look like Kim Kardashian. Not round my manor anyway. And if the women in our street did look like her, I would probably be too shy to go up and *rabbit* to them. Real women have love handles. Accept the fact. Deal with it. Move on.

I don't expect women to be perfect in much the same way, as I'm not. My waistline is like Tottenham High Road on a Saturday night – it needs continual policing. I also have a boil on my bottom, but we don't need to go there. Real women are not any less desirable than their airbrushed counterparts – and, they have the elusive quality that Kim does not – they are attainable.

BY ROGER MCCARTNEY 27

MEN ARE FROM MARS
I'M FROM TOTTENHAM

During my life, several of my female acquaintances have gone on about being over-weight, when there was absolutely nothing wrong with them. Trips to Highbury Leisure Centre and splodging about down at Wapping Old Stairs, have had to be aborted or she will turn up looking like Lawrence of Arabia.

Sometimes women will even request, "Don't have a *Butcher's* at me!" when they take their clothes off. Well how is that going to work then? Am I supposed to move in for a spot of lovemaking by using the handy Braille signposting provided?

It seems to me that Spurs women feel they have to attain stick insect like qualities. Are you having a *Turkish*? These women look positively underfed. I want to take them home, not to get in their *Alan Whickers*, but to give them some decent nosh or maybe take them up the Pie and Mash shop. Under-nourishment is not an attractive quality, you know?

BY ROGER MCCARTNEY 28

MEN ARE FROM MARS
I'M FROM TOTTENHAM

I am not going to tell you *porkies* and say that I find obesity attractive; I personally don't although some Spurs men do. There is a limit. However, curves attract Spurs men. And the circle line is my favourite tube line too. You see, **we are programmed to fancy you,** rounded tummy or not. Although, I must be honest and state that the law of diminishing returns will occur once the acceptable level of curviness has been reached. But this level is **way beyond what most Spurs women would think.**

<u>Secret #5:</u> Euston, We Have a Problem: Spurs Man Is Rubbish at DIY.

I was down in Spurs tube station at midnight the other night, when I suddenly had a thought. It's a fact of life, that men, born within the sound of the Lane, are expected to be naturals at DIY. We are not the men from Del Monte. We are the men from Del's café in the High Road, so get on and fix it mate!

As soon as something in the gaff goes pear-shaped, or the pipes in the downstairs khazi begin crying out to have a nice little timber unit fashioned around them, then the male of the partnership will become firmly fixed in the gaze of expectation. In my experience, this supposition, that we men are inherently able to do DIY, is one of the downsides to having the XY chromosomes.

BY ROGER MCCARTNEY 30

MEN ARE FROM MARS
I'M FROM TOTTENHAM

Woman think that all men are naturals at DIY. Let me take you by the hand and lead you through the streets of Spurs. I'll show you something to make you change your mind.

Even though London history was fashioned by men from the manufacturing industry, we are not all master craftsmen here on the Lea. In fact, some of us are craftsmanship-challenged; but then the table from IKEA I've just assembled, cack-handedly, back-to-front, kind of gives it away.

Of course, our women could and should call in the experts, but to allow this would be an admission of failure as a man. The very thought of another fella coming in to do a job when we have sufficient limbs and fingers, would be the DIY equivalent of being cuckolded.

The reasons for this expectation of Spurs men lie in our caveman roots, when DIY was first

BY ROGER MCCARTNEY 31

invented to ensure survival of the fittest. We sat in our caves, fashioning crude objects out of wood and stone, while the woman prepared roast mammoth for lunch.

Two million years later and things have progressed. Rather than worship the moon, we now have the ability to play golf on it. However, I am still sat here attempting to fashion crude objects out of wood and stone.

Modern day DIY is primarily to ensure the amusement of the fattest. Success at it feeds directly into our self-esteem and, more importantly, feeds directly into the esteem our women have for us. Our qualities as the provider may be under examination; the provider of shelving units, which do not slope, that is.

At Highbury Grove, I just didn't get woodwork and metalwork. Sure, I was inventive with excuses, but I wasn't so resourceful when it came to shape the materials into anything

 BY ROGER MCCARTNEY 32

remotely useful. No wonder I used to skive off home to watch afternoon telly. I didn't foresee that one day my life's purpose would come down to the alignment of two holes in the wall. I also didn't foresee the Headmaster would tan my backside for skiving. But that's another story.

Because I never listened at school and haven't since been to University to get a degree in engineering, my aptitude for DIY is severely restricted, and has cursed me all my life. I was 32 before I owned a screwdriver, and I was 35 before I used it. My toolbox was stolen once, and I was secretly relieved. The Missus has cocked a blind'un to my uselessness, because she is always going to have a requirement for someone to assemble the thirty-two flat packs she orders from MFI, useless or not.

The only thing that *will* come naturally to me when things start to go wrong will be the expletives, once I've nailed my hand to the table a few times. Indeed, I will be a lot more

BY ROGER MCCARTNEY 33

MEN ARE FROM MARS
I'M FROM TOTTENHAM

inventive in the creation of profanities than in the creation of furniture.

I will become so irritated, after stabbing my thumb for the third time, that I'll destroy the very object I am trying to construct. This defeats the purpose of DIY, which is to build things - not to demolish them, halfway through the process, once you've part-crucified yourself. I will drop the hammer on my toes as routinely as I drop H's. I will then proceed to swear and cuss with more voracity than John Terry. Now we'll see who's bad!

I suppose my ineptitude could be hereditary as I remember that in my childhood, back when Martin Chivers was god and men were men and sheep were scared; the old man always used to saw into the table and routinely electrocute himself. He used to get the right hump. When they were giving brains out, he thought they said 'trains' and he asked for a slow one. Was he

BY ROGER MCCARTNEY 34

MEN ARE FROM MARS
I'M FROM TOTTENHAM

daft, you ask? Yes: he married me muvver, I reply.

On Completion of tasks, I will expect much praise and promises of nooky. Otherwise the next time she asks me to put a picture up I might just answer in the true spirit of DIY and say, **"Do it yourself, gel!"**

Secret #6: Spurs Man Has Difficulty Saying "I Love You, Gel."

Spurs men are not very emotional. Apparently. Apart from when Ricky Villa scored the winner in the 81 replay. Then we were emotional.

This allegation from the fair sex, of our un-emotional-ness, arises from our reluctance to say the sentence that can mean so much to a woman. And that sentence is not **"Shall I empty the bin?"**

No, the group of words that causes us the greatest consternation and the one I personally have difficulty marshalling to my lips is: **"I love you, gel."**

A Spurs man will enthuse "I love Dele Ali: He was fantastic against West Ham and he

BY ROGER MCCARTNEY 36

compliments Kane perfectly; Ali breaks up play and simply plays the ball short allowing Kane to probe higher up the pitch" or 'I love Pochettino – best manager we ever had'. But ask him to use 'love' in a statement of endearment towards his life-partner and it becomes a word that is almost impossible to say.

'Sorry' is a word that is easy to say. I will spray 'sorry' around liberally, all day if necessary. Each time I bump into someone: 'sorry'. Each time I tread on someone's *plates*: 'sorry'. Each time she says, 'You really hurt me': 'sorry'.

'Sorry' is the catch-all remedy that makes everything better. It is instant verbal healing. "Sorry, we threw away a two-goal lead". In football, when the trainer applies the magic spray to the injured player's leg: that is the aerosol form of 'sorry'.

Just as I reserve the wearing of my 1991 FA Cup winning retro strip for Sunday best, I will

BY ROGER MCCARTNEY 37

keep back the phrase **"I love you, gel"** for special occasions too.

I <u>will</u> only say 'I love you' when I am backed into a corner and a proclamation of fondness is the only way out. In partnership-threatening situations, such as an argument, the statement can save the day. If utilised correctly, it can be the injection of adrenaline that an ailing or stagnant relationship needs.

Sometimes, I will use the **'I love you'** card tactically; to get what I want, smooth things over, or to put points in the Affection Bank.

Besides, relationship protocol demands you must sprinkle the phrase into the mix occasionally, otherwise your boyfriend skills may be deemed to suck. If you are not careful you are then heading for the resultant **'you never say you love me'** discussion – and no one wants to go down that *frog and toad.* Been there, done that, cleaned the blood off my t-shirt. "You never say

BY ROGER MCCARTNEY 38

you love me" will inevitably lead on to "you never express yourself." At this point, I may well 'express' myself: by throttling her.

So why are the three words of adoration, so difficult? Firstly, because **'I love you'**, is coming from a place deep down – deeper than White Hart Lane tube station. By reaching down to find this sentiment, you are opening a duct directly into your soul. Good stuff, such as **'I love you'** can come out, but equally, bad stuff, such as **'I hate you',** can get in. Best to keep the entrance to this channel always blocked by triviality .

Secondly, **'I love you'** is an admission of weakness. It goes against the manly grain. I may as well say "Please walk all over me... and don't forget to lock up, afterwards!"

As a Spurs man, I must be tough, not weak; it's part of the job description. I don't do weakness, me. Weakness is not going to protect against the sabre-toothed tiger when it comes bounding

BY ROGER MCCARTNEY 39

into the cave or nowadays, when the burglar comes creeping into the house late at night. Perhaps I can persuade him to put the metal bar down by telling him I love *him*?

The next time your man has fallen short of the regulation thirty expressions of devotion per month, don't berate him; treat him kindly. He's an emotionally stunted cripple for good reason.

Tell him that *you* love *him*, for as far as the 'I love you' declaration goes **I think it's far nicer to receive than it is to give.**

<u>Secret #7</u>: Question: What Do Spurs Geezers Find More Annoying Than Arsenal? Answer: Last Orders and Shopping.

I know 'Jesus saves' and all that – Kane gets the rebound by the way – but If Jesus had been a Londoner, the last supper would have been pie and mash. And if Jesus had been a woman, she'd have taken them all up Oxford Street.

The next relationship I get into; I'm going to find out from the outset if we're shopping-soul mates. Apart from needing to know if we are suited in the bedroom department, I need to know if we are suited in the department-store department.

BY ROGER MCCARTNEY 41

MEN ARE FROM MARS
I'M FROM TOTTENHAM

If we are going to be spending a good proportion of 'us time' in John Lewis, particularly in the acquisition of new clothes for *her*, it makes sense to find out if we're John-Lewis-compatible. The couple that shops together stays together. Although this theory is cobblers as she will no doubt keep slouching off.

My preference is for the SAS style of shopping; get in, get the purchase, and get out again in as quick a time as possible. This renders me practically useless as good female company. If I could, I would even chuck in a stun grenade to facilitate the encounter. Ideally, I would be so quick that even the CCTV would not pick me up, which is good, as then I can't be prosecuted for the grenade-throwing incident.

Of course, the missus will out-shop me every time. Even when we are in B & Q, having a *Butcher's* at power-saws, she is enjoying the experience more than I am.

 BY ROGER MCCARTNEY 42

MEN ARE FROM MARS
I'M FROM TOTTENHAM

The only time I genuinely enjoy shopping is when we are food shopping in Sainsbury's, Northumberland Park in the new stadium complex. It says on the job-specification of a man that he is the number one provider – so there is a certain amount of role fulfilment to be had for the man, in the attainment of the weekly provisions.

I find clothes shopping a far more irksome task. It is a lot quicker, and fulfilling, watching grass grow - and at least you get to sit down a bit. I don't like anything, apart from The London Marathon, which lasts half a day or more. She is far better to go with her mum, her daughter, Chirpy the Cockerel, or someone, anyone, other than me.

My standing-up span is severely limited, and I will immediately collapse, upon entering a shop, into the nearest chair. You will usually find me in the footwear department not checking out the loafers – but instead - loafing on the chairs

BY ROGER MCCARTNEY 43

provided, watching *Final Score*, to see how Tottenham got on, if possible.

Buying clothes is like decorating the lounge - it's decoration of the human torso. Embellishment is best left to the female. Just as I wouldn't contest her selection of sequinned cushions, from the market, I also wouldn't interfere in her choice of frock.

After she's spent an hour trying them all on in *New Look* she will breeze out of the shop, saying that nothing suited. I am not so foolish to think that we won't be back before the day is out to pick up the outfit that she secretly liked.

The amount of time I have spent waiting outside changing rooms. You don't get that time back. And if you did get it back, God with his sense of irony would probably allocate you a few more hours in *John Lewis* or something.

Spurs women are at home in clothing outlets. Simple as. I suspect they all have that inner

BY ROGER MCCARTNEY 44

catwalk model in them trying to get out, even if the audience consists of only a disgruntled partner and a mirror.

The upside for me is that I get to see her in various stages of dress and undress. And as an unexpected bonus, I may get to see other women in various stages of dress and undress, as I hang around the changing rooms. Legitimately this time.

And if I grunt enough encouraging approvals, I might get treated to the treasured *Ruby Murray* afterwards. I'm absolutely *Hank Marvin* after me shopping trip.

Forget *Dorothy Perkins.* A Chicken Tikka Masala. **Now that's my idea of shopping! Sweet as a nut mate!**

BY ROGER MCCARTNEY 45

<u>Secret #8</u>: Two Things That Spurs Men like to Avoid: The Black Death and Ladettes. Oh, and Arsenal Fans

As an Oyster card-carrying, red-blooded Spurs fella, I like to meet women across a wide spectrum of different types and women. Providing they are carrying the necessary double x chromosomal pattern, then they're in. Simple as that.

However, there is one type of woman that I like to give a wide berth to, when assessing potential partners. These are, of course, Spurs women that delight in copying the behaviour of Spurs men: **Ladettes**. Absolute nause they are. Gutted, when I meet them. I well like to avoid them, if at all possible.

BY ROGER MCCARTNEY 46

MEN ARE FROM MARS
I'M FROM TOTTENHAM

Ladettes are often more laddish than the lads they are trying to replicate. Only one problem Euston: **we don't like it**. If we wanted a female companion to be a geezer, we would just simply place an ad for a geezer. Once women start acting all masculine, they neutralise their sexuality, which in turn neutralises their attractiveness. The whole attraction of women to us is built upon the assumption that they are just that: WOMEN. Once the lines of gender become blurred you might just as well have a game of snooker with the Missus and go to bed with Gazza.

Ladettes alarm us because they out-male us. They play football. They like to drink pints, laugh raucously and stub out cigarettes on our hands. They are often better fighters than we are, and, can out drink us. What's the point in having one for a girlfriend? It's like having a date with the Yid Army.

BY ROGER MCCARTNEY 47

MEN ARE FROM MARS
I'M FROM TOTTENHAM

In the bedroom, they also try to out-do us by being more macho and throwing us around the room a little. And that's just the foreplay! That's not on! We like to be in charge in the bedroom or at very least be kept informed as to what's happening.

I once knew a woman that turned out to be this type. Came on a bit *Hong Kong,* like. I met her in El Comandante and she proceeded to act as if she was the Commandant. If I'd known what the night of wrestling was going to be like, I would have asked her to go gentle with me, as it was my first time with a sexually aggressive woman. And last. Hopefully. I would have rather gawn to the Flower Show. Or Chelsea away. Somewhere, anywhere than that.

When me and her went up the *apples and pears* back at my place, well, it all kicked off didn't it? It all started to go *Pete Tong* from there really. She proceeded to bounce us off the walls and tug us in places I didn't even know were official

 BY ROGER MCCARTNEY 48

tugging zones, like. She was asking all the questions, but I didn't have any of the answers. It was awful. The next morning, I enquired if she knew the whereabouts of my testicles. On receiving her answer, I collected them from the far-flung corners of the room and fled. I swear on my mum's life, never again mate.

I was lucky to escape with my life, not to mention my *Orchestras*. It was worse than a visit to White hart Lane.

I am still not sure if she qualified as a ladette or just an out and out nutter. And as I have been proven to be a nutter-magnet, it was probably the latter.

Read my lips: We men don't like women to be more sexually voracious than we are. Voracity is our job. Comes with the turf. We are the Spurs men. Cockerels on our *Dickys* and all that. We've still got the Blitz spirit. It's a Spurs thing. Good old Spurs.

BY ROGER MCCARTNEY 49

MEN ARE FROM MARS
I'M FROM TOTTENHAM

You can call me old-school, but we men will do all the necessary bouncing and tugging, thank you very much! Over-zealousness on the part of the female is guaranteed to kill 99% of all household erections; and If I wanted that sort of interaction with a female, I would enter the Highbury and Islington mixed sumo-wrestling championships.

In my view, women are supposed to act demurely and flutter their eyelids as they blush at the very mention of the bedroom. Not turn into Ricky Savage on a bad Barnet day, the moment the bedroom door is locked. I find that ever so *Mariah Carey,* as would any red-blooded male.

The only woman I want then, **is me mum.**

BY ROGER MCCARTNEY 50

<u>Secret #9:</u> What Makes Spurs Men Blub? Apart from Losing and Tube Strikes?

Ozzy's knees may or may not still be all trembly – we can but speculate – but me: I didn't do sensitivity until I was twenty-one. That was the day the sort with the golden *Barnet*, from over Tottenham Hale way, decided it was over. Then I became sensitive.

Growing up, I had always adhered to the Big Boys Don't Cry rule. You were not allowed to blub except when Spurs got knocked out of Europe. So quite often then!

But from the age of five, I was expected to be striving towards manhood, and not bawling like a baby. The predominant parental attitude was:

BY ROGER MCCARTNEY 51

MEN ARE FROM MARS
I'M FROM TOTTENHAM

'cry me a river and build me a bridge, mate'. Not a Stamford Bridge, obviously. That's Roman's job.

By adulthood, I was an automaton, devoid of feeling altogether. If I so much as showed a nanosecond of emotion, amid my peer group, then I would receive the punishment of being jeered to death.

But this new adult pain, initiated by the honey-Barnetted one, was altogether different. The sadness was so great, that the emotion had nowhere else to go other than to explode out through my tear ducts. And I didn't give a *monkey's* what the peer group thought.

She was the person who first tweaked my crying nerve. In our short time together, we shared a crash course in love. When our love inevitably *did* crash, the lesson became 'how to cry', for she had given me good reason to.

BY ROGER MCCARTNEY 52

MEN ARE FROM MARS
I'M FROM TOTTENHAM

The mourning period for that relationship lasted longer than the relationship itself. I was gutted. Kleenex was looking to sponsor me, and my mates were looking to give me a good kicking. "Are ya coming down the Shelf Saturday, mate? She's only a gel!" they said.

"You wait, you'll see," I snivelled, and sure enough, one by one, in the forthcoming months they were all struck down by the heartbreak-virus. It was my turn to gloat and provide the anti-virus: alcohol and profound slogans – among them: "she's only a gel!"

My life was suddenly as empty as Bill Nicholson Way on a non-match day. Professional counselling could have helped, but I embarked on a more immediate remedy: drinking myself silly. Drink only made things worse, and then I really *did* need counselling – for alcohol addiction. I used to bell *Alcoholics Anonymous* so regularly, the guy, who was getting pulled out of *The Lord*

MEN ARE FROM MARS
I'M FROM TOTTENHAM

Palmerston each time to come on the *doggan*, was getting the right zig.

I was like that bird on the telly, Judy: I needed a new *Richard* and quick. After a few weeks of a woman-less life, I would have been happy to take out an attractive wildebeest for pie and mash, rather than go on my *Jack*. And after a few more weeks, it didn't even have to be an attractive one.

The decline into being a wuss, accelerated as I got older and I have now even been reduced to blubbing now when *we score a goal* instead of the more traditional, tear-inducing, conceding of a goal. It's a happy form of crying, although to protect the man-status I need to sob as inconspicuously as possible. I will deliver each droplet down my cheek as inconspicuously as I deliver my h's. I was not expecting to blub for England when I sat down this afternoon in front of the tele. That's Gazza's job.

BY ROGER MCCARTNEY 54

MEN ARE FROM MARS
I'M FROM TOTTENHAM

Although the letting down of the manly guard is regrettable, I find that sobbing in front of a woman can be beneficial too. It may result in much female nurturing and soothing. As a youngster, a gashed knee would result in the immediate requirement for mum. Now, I run to her-indoors, retaining as much macho poise as possible even if tears are streaming.

This interaction is like saying to her, "You take over the reins for a moment whilst I have this mini-breakdown like, and then we'll resume as normal." She may be pleased she's chosen a compassionate human being for a companion – or riled that she's chosen a cry-baby. Failing that, and I'm on the blower to mum.

I don't know why I cry. Maybe it was dates to all those European nights when we just couldn't seem to get nowhere. Maybe I'm still a bit of a miserable git from those days - with 'unhappy' rubber-stamped on my soul. Or maybe I still miss Goldilocks. She was the one that released

BY ROGER MCCARTNEY 55

the dam that had been waiting to burst all those years, and then even the London Barrier cocked a deaf 'un when it came to hold back the tears. All those years of stubbing my toe, having my virility questioned in the changing rooms, and England getting knocked out early doors in the World Cup. That was a huge back-catalogue of tears!

We Spurs men are only human; you know? If you cut us, do we not bleed white and navy blue? **And we are likely to blub a bit too!**

MEN ARE FROM MARS
I'M FROM TOTTENHAM

<u>Secret #10:</u> Question: Do North London Geezers Cheat? Answer: Did Jack the Ripper Have Issues?

Nothing is certain in London but expense. But another thing that is certain in North London, is that men cheat.

But the good news is that not all men do. Here in this north London multi-cultural hotchpotch, we are made of explosive stuff. The 'Hotspurs' part of our name is derived from a knight for Gawd's sake. That being said, we do not necessarily have the fortitude of a Knight when it comes to being unfaithful and neither do, we all have the necessary *bottle*.

That's the good news. The bad news is that the rest of the Spurs male population are

BY ROGER MCCARTNEY 57

actively cheating, thinking of cheating or would cheat if an opportunity presents itself. The Spurs brotherhood will angrily deny it, but then we claim the right to tell porkies, in case we incriminate ourselves.

I personally am between cheats at the moment, as you need a primary relationship in order to cheat on it with a secondary one.

So why do Spurs men cheat? I'm not going to tell you that it lies in our evolutionary cavegeezer roots. That's *Jackson Pollocks!* That excuse is *so* two million years ago! However, it *is* one of three perfectly valid reasons to explain our propensity to roam.

Firstly, as males, our instinct is to spread our genes around as much as possible. Even as far as away as Walthamstow. I mean, Walthamstow is so far east, they're practically French anyway. Man's penchant for procreation is how the human race has flourished, indeed over-flourished, since our earliest beginnings. If

BY ROGER MCCARTNEY 58

women were in charge of initiating procreation: the human population would be about the size that London was in 1300: one square mile.

Back in the day, and we're talking pre-Alan Gilzean here, man needed to sow his seed as much as possible to ensure the survival and advancement of the human race. This means that today, the need to procreate with more than one partner still resides deep down in our psyche – and doesn't go away, even if we go and lie down in a darkened room. Unfortunately, we are hard-wired to have an eye for the next new partner, even when we are perfectly content with the current one.

Secondly, it doesn't take a lot to make us men feel inadequate and that's exactly how we feel when we haven't had enough partners in life. This feeling of inadequacy is nature's way of telling us to sleep about more.

Inside every man - even those with geeky-façade - there is a serial womaniser struggling

BY ROGER MCCARTNEY 59

to get out. This womaniser is itching to be let out and once free, will proceed to cruise about the High Road and pull women in the time-honoured fashion.

Finally, there is the thrill of the chase. The need to clinch the deal goes with the testosterone filled territory. We are like salesmen, who don't feel they can rest until they've got another signature on the dotted line. Remember Spurs men are very much chase-orientated, and the thrill derived from it. We want success. We always have. This drives us on to push up the numbers and hit our self-appointed targets.

Even with these pre-conditions working against us, Spurs men can and will stay faithful - unless a certain final condition occurs that of opportunity. Without it, we are nothing. It is written in our chromosomal make-up that we cannot resist a sexual opportunity. Even if you

BY ROGER MCCARTNEY 60

MEN ARE FROM MARS
I'M FROM TOTTENHAM

are the offspring of ol' Muvver Teresa May, you are going to be sorely tempted.

Spurs men are not the only love-rats either – it's just that we get all the headlines in *The Sun*. Some of my best women friends have been love-ratesses, and worse still, some have been my partners.

The problem with evolutionary heredity is that it takes so darn long to shake it out of our system. So, don't expect any change in man's inclination to be cheats for the next million years or so. But don't worry, **after that, we may settle down!**

BY ROGER MCCARTNEY 61

MEN ARE FROM MARS
I'M FROM TOTTENHAM

<u>Secret #11:</u> Spurs Men Don't do Plastic. Unless It's Oyster.

There is a saying that when you are tired of the Spurs, you are tired of life. But there is one thing that Spurs fans will never tire of, however, and that is boobs. Oh, and being the best team in Europe. We proved that the other week by beating the best team in Europe.

Boobs are not just a matter of life or death to Spurs man. They are more important than that. Maybe not as important as getting a new Spurs top each August, but boobs still rate highly on the must-have scale; or, I should say, the must-view scale. And as you can tell from the fact that our peepers are on permanent ogling standby, we are obsessed by cleavage here in N17.

BY ROGER MCCARTNEY 62

MEN ARE FROM MARS
I'M FROM TOTTENHAM

You will never want to be *brown bread* if there are boobs around this manor. Cleavage is important because it sends an inaudible message saying, 'I am Woman', and this message is only discernible by male *mince pies*.

Just as women like to accessorise, so do we Spurs men. When fine dining up the *Billy Nick* or even somewhere fancier, we like to accessorise with a pretty woman on the arm, or even just a woman with that minimum male requirement: a pulse.

Things change, as you get older. When I was a young 'un, we used to play Knock Down Ginger. And I don't mean we used to chuck bean bags at De Bruyne. The rules of the game were you had to knock on someone's door and run away. Nowadays it's called Parcelforce.

When I was young, I longed for a woman with a magnificent chest. Now I am older, I long for a

BY ROGER MCCARTNEY 63

woman with a personality... as well as a magnificent chest. A *Richard* once said to me that I hadn't noticed her *thrupennies* at all. This I thought was a trifle unfair, as that was the main thing my *minces* had clocked.

So, with that in mind, you might think that if you asked a man if he liked implants it would be like asking a child if he wanted an extra bag of sweets. The answer would be somewhere in the 'are you having a *Turkish* my son?' range.

True enough, Spurs men do like an enormous surgically enhanced bosom, but our fascination is in a sort of freakish sideshow type of way.

It's a little-known fact, other than in man-cliques, that Spurs man will always prefer natural to the surgically improved counterparts. To the true Spurs male, implants are like people that speak fluent mockney: there is something infinitely false and unnatural about them. Or am I missing the point?

BY ROGER MCCARTNEY 64

MEN ARE FROM MARS
I'M FROM TOTTENHAM

Enhancement of the bust is fine, but wanting to attain Katie Price proportions, well that's just *Mariah Carey*. I would be afraid, very afraid if I found myself within the same room as that gel and her *Bristols*. For a start, I wouldn't know where to look - as her bust will have taken up the entire available panorama. I mean is there any real need to have a bosom that big? I believe that if Katy Price and her *thrupennies* really are intent on world domination; I say, "You go gel!"

If Jordan *were* my woman, in some sort of parallel universe, her chest would obviously give me an inferiority complex. And, being a Spurs man, I don't do inferiority! Cockerels on our chests, us. Spurs conquered the world - first team to do the double in modern times - and then brought back the trophies to the Lane to prove it.

BY ROGER MCCARTNEY 65

MEN ARE FROM MARS
I'M FROM TOTTENHAM

It is not knowledge that is power in the male/female dynamic - it is cleavage. A woman armed with impressive breasts can cause us to act right *Radio Rental.* If I am not careful, I will soon be doing even madder things such as gleefully picking up the tab for a *Ruby.*

As one of the thousands of T.H.F.C men, doubling up as Baywatch fans each on Saturday teatime, I can vouch that implants can have a certain surface appeal. *Sexton Blake* or not, Pamela's still dining out on her assets even now, or more recently, falling down *Brahms and Liszt* on them.

Contrary to female opinion, when I see a woman with implants, my tongue does not roll out like an elasticised red carpet. The official Spurs geezer perspective is this: Cleavage does not have to be Wembley-like to be desirable. Small is also good. And have I mentioned how underrated middle-sized is? From our point of

BY ROGER MCCARTNEY 66

view, there is no right or wrong with chests. It's all good underneath the hood bruv!

Remember: A bad day at the Spurs is better than a good day somewhere else. **And it's like that with breasts too.**

BY ROGER MCCARTNEY 67

Secret #12: Why Does Spurs Man Always Have to Make the First Move?

Glory glory Tottenham Hotspur, but why is it here at the Spurs that it is always the man that must make the first move? It's an absolute nause, it really is. But if he doesn't, he may as well de-evolve into a single cell organism, able to replicate only with himself. He may as well go off and have a *Jodrell,* for that is all the attention he will get from the opposite sex. He might as well be *brown bread* my son.

Now that I am firmly back in the dating arena, once again I am cast as the cheetah stalking the gazelle. Right predator I am. As I leave my phone number on the *jam jar* outside the Benwell Road Co-op, that belongs to the pretty woman I have been admiring for the last few weeks, I feel as though I am the Cheetah. The

BY ROGER MCCARTNEY 68

only difference in this scenario to the African bush, is that this cheetah wants to take Miss Gazelle out for a *Ruby* – not for her to be in the *Ruby*!

But for once, I would like to have a day off from doing predatory. Blimey, just for once, I would like to have a go at the gazelle role. It would be sweet as a nut to be on the receiving end of a pursuit for a change.

I learnt the lesson of 'faint heart never won fair sort' early in life. But ignoring sort altogether? Madness! This is not a successful tactic for the lone male to follow. You might as well sign your own single warrant.

It must be decreed somewhere in the Magna Carta that it is a woman's human right to have males-a-plenty chasing her. The last sort - that wasn't Old Bill - that came after me voluntarily, was when I was eight years old at Drayton Park Primary. It was round about the time Charlie

BY ROGER MCCARTNEY 69

George was scoring *that* goal, our first double year.

She had sweet ponytails and used to pursue me round the playground in an innocent game of kiss-chase. Naturally, I was so adept, and fast at running, that I was never caught. As the game preceded my learning to kiss by about five years, thank goodness I escaped; otherwise, I would have been in all kinds of trouble! The roles reversed soon after, and it became the chasee's turn to become chaser, and has been ever since.

Only Spurs geezers that have an uncanny resemblance to Messrs Pitt, Law or Clooney, don't have to sing so hard for their romantic suppers, and generally can expect to scoop up the phone numbers, without effort. But everyone else has to work jolly hard to get female attention.

Women expect to be courted, simple as. But sometimes, I would prefer to live in a parallel

BY ROGER MCCARTNEY 70

universe – where the women chase us. Then I could flutter my eyelashes and rebuff advances with the tried and trusted mugging-off line: "Nah fanks, ta very much. I'm washing me *Barnet* tonight."

Spurs men also have to attain the necessary balance with our predatory tactics. Come on too *Hong Kong* and you might scare the Spurs out of her. Too laid back and you will have to go and join the back of the queue and wait until your turn comes around again.

One of life's burning questions is why is the aesthetically challenged man is going out with the rather more aesthetically blessed woman. Well it's simple: it is because he asked. Yes, that's right. He drew in his belly, pumped himself up and had the necessary bottle to ask. Go on my son. Get In. And she said yes, because she didn't have anything better to do this side of the next ice age.

BY ROGER MCCARTNEY 71

MEN ARE FROM MARS
I'M FROM TOTTENHAM

All women have downtime in their schedules when no other Spurs men are asking. This is when a geek masquerading as Mr Nice Guy can get through. I know all about this; I have got through several geek-force fields during my time on this planet.

If I'd known at the outset it was going to be so difficult to catch a woman, I would have let the pony-tailed one at Drayton Park catch *me* a few more times. Maybe then, I would be a better kisser as well. So come on women, spice it up a bit, nah what I mean? **Why don't you chase *us* for a change?**

BY ROGER MCCARTNEY 72

MEN ARE FROM MARS
I'M FROM TOTTENHAM

<u>Secret #13:</u> Crikey! Spurs Geezers Fall in Love More Often Than Kerry Katona.

Would you *Adam and Eve* that the first week "I love you" was said to me once? It was just after the League Cup win in 2008, when we beat Chelsea. Straight up! After picking myself up off the floor and not wishing to appear rude, I said it right back. Then, after exchanging the mutual love-vow with haste, we then spent the next few years unravelling the commitment, at leisure.

However, such an early pledge remains a predominantly Spurs-male gambit. It is one of our characteristics, when we go all starry-eyed over a new starlet in our lives; we are unable to hold back. But, at what point is it safe to first

BY ROGER MCCARTNEY 73

tell a woman of your love without scaring the Spurs out of her?

The need to clinch the deal goes with the testosterone-filled territory. We are like car salesmen: we don't feel we can rest until we've got another signature on the dotted line. Remember Spurs men are very much chase-orientated, and the thrill derived from it.

In the first few days of a burgeoning relationship, there comes a point when it is necessary for the man to clinch the deal. In olden days, we would just club you over the head and point to the nearest cave. Now, because we are a little bit more technologically advanced, we may use an I phone to text it, but the message remains the same: we like you and we want you to move into our cave. Or more likely, can we move into your clean, tidy cave please?

Pitch this message too soon and the relationship may self-destruct. A premature utterance of 'I

BY ROGER MCCARTNEY 74

MEN ARE FROM MARS
I'M FROM TOTTENHAM

love you, gel' will cause a woman to run for the hills just as surely as Vinnie Jones turning up outside the stadium for a meet and greet.

I once knew a woman. I knew immediately she was not from Spurs as she spoke English far too well. There was an indication of her not being from here, as she had more rabbit than Sainsbury. Most people in London don't talk to you. She did.

Our first kiss had gone smoothly, and her bruised toe was recovering nicely from where I had stood on it. Love-bites had been exchanged and horizontal relations were on the horizon. The schoolboy error was not, in the note thanking her for a lovely evening - it was in the added PS - that I was falling in love with her.

Naturally, Miss Non-Reciprocal spat us out quicker than an undercooked kebab. Blimey, she was right taters towards me after *I-love-you-gate*. She got the right hump. When I belled her

BY ROGER MCCARTNEY 75

MEN ARE FROM MARS
I'M FROM TOTTENHAM

a few days later, to enquire why she had moved back to Wapping, she mugged me off with the line: "It's because you said you love me".

Oh, I see! That explains it. Maybe the government can get illegal immigrants to go back home, by telling them that **I** have fallen in love with them?

"You never tell a woman you love her. Never!" exclaimed my best mate. Whilst, I noted his comments, I couldn't help noticing too, the lack of female companionship. I also wondered about the colour of the sky in his world. But I noticed he did have Sky in his world, so I vowed to be round next Sunday to watch the Spurs on it!

Obviously, my ex-lover, thought I was some sort of plonker who gets his kicks from falling hopelessly for women after one date. Well, she was about as spot on as she could get; for I *am* that plonker.

BY ROGER MCCARTNEY 76

MEN ARE FROM MARS
I'M FROM TOTTENHAM

I had acted like a young'un in the game of love, which, being only 42 at the time, was understandable. I was only trying to bring her closer, not make her flee Spurs altogether.

We do delude ourselves though. No matter how much I jolly well force myself - I can't fall in love with someone I met just two days ago. It's that old devil called lust – masquerading as love again. We're chasing the unicorn, I guess. But the unicorn doesn't exist. It's like Leeds trying to get back in the Prem: it's a dream. It's not going to happen.

Sometimes it is good to get the **'I love you'** out during the first week, meaningless or not; weed out the timewasters. Nah wot I mean? If she walks, then so be it; Wapping is very nice, I hear. Down by the river. Nice pub there: *Town of Ramsgate.*

In fact, I'm thinking of starting my next relationship with asking **"Hello, I love you!**

BY ROGER MCCARTNEY 77

MEN ARE FROM MARS
I'M FROM TOTTENHAM

Won't you tell me your name." Or was that the Doors?

BY ROGER MCCARTNEY 78

MEN ARE FROM MARS
I'M FROM TOTTENHAM

<u>Secret #14:</u> Would You *Adam and Eve* It? Spurs Men Don't Do Home Improvement.

You can call me a pessimist if you like, but I fear it won't end well. It's that time of year again – when wallpaper sample books appear, and Spurs blokes want to take cover behind the sofa that they soon be asked to reposition. No, it's not Sadiq Khan coming around door to door; It's time to re-decorate, my son.

The reason for the process is simple. Most couples desire the biggest and best property they can afford. Ideally, they want a palatial residence, but cannot always get one because of restrictions in affluence. It is therefore necessary to achieve the palatial effect in their modest home: by decorating the hell out of it.

BY ROGER MCCARTNEY 79

MEN ARE FROM MARS
I'M FROM TOTTENHAM

Each gender's strengths will be played to in the decoration process. Female brain will be used to conceptualise, whilst male brawn will be utilised during implementation. No doubt, Spurs men will have an aptitude for DIY. The fashioning of items out of wood, stone and iron appeals directly to our inner cavegeezer and our Spurs roots. But decorating should be left to the professionals or failing that: women.

Sure, Spurs men can point a drill at the wall and move seemingly insurmountable pieces of furniture, just as efficiently as Samson used to, but women have ownership of the embellishment skills.

The Female of the species is more deadly than the male – at the arranging of the sequinned cushions, and the placing of the yin/yang ornaments, picked up from Kings Road. Women are, by instinct, nest makers and therefore by extension – nest decorators. It is an innate thing.

BY ROGER MCCARTNEY 80

MEN ARE FROM MARS
I'M FROM TOTTENHAM

Lea-side men, in their chromosomal make-up, have deficiencies in certain genes that inhibit their decorating ability, particularly the taste gene. They can recognise colours but are unable to co-ordinate them. Blue is the colour, and sod everything else! They are also deficient in the try-to-look-interested gene. Women, however, have both genes in abundance.

Spurs men do not attempt this at home! Put the lava lamp down and move away from the net curtains!

Furnishing is a subject that I have always filed in the mental 'don't-care-about' drawer. Not my circus, not my monkeys. I'm the one who thought *décor* was a type of decaffeinated coffee, remember? And why scatter cushions? Why not just place them sensibly?

In most couples, women are allowed *carte blanche* to furnish. For Health & Safety

BY ROGER MCCARTNEY 81

purposes, it is sensible for a man to interfere or question her about her decorating decisions, only if he is wearing a hard *titfer*. Furthermore, failure to complete tasks assigned to him, satisfactorily, may call his masculinity into question.

Spurs men are shackled by the fact that they told *porkies* early in the relationship about their interest in home improvement. That was a load of *Jacksons* and a big mistake too, for now the refurbishment genie is out of the bottle; you must now feed the voracious appetite that women have for consistently transforming the dwelling space.

Decorating the gaff is like building the new stadium: once you finish, you need to start all over. This perpetual decorating treadmill is virtually guaranteed, if you have sleepwalked into allowing your partner to be the Project Manager. My own irrelevant view is that it is far

BY ROGER MCCARTNEY 82

MEN ARE FROM MARS
I'M FROM TOTTENHAM

better not to start any work on the house in the first place and live in abject squalor.

She may seduce you into watching home improvement TV programs, in the hope that you will be inspired. You may well be inspired - to flee. The will to live will also slowly begin to drain from your body as a new schedule of tasks is assigned to you.

A good way to make up for the lack of new furniture coming in, is to get more creative with existing furniture, by re-arranging the layout. A sofa moved over there; a rug moved over here. This lulls you into a feeling of improvement, without the expense.

Careful, Spurs fans, that it is not *you* that is spoiling the ambience of the place - otherwise *you* might well be re-positioned. Outside the front door. Then you will see what her ultimate interior plan was all along. Maybe it was that '*Chez Nous*' **should simply become, '*Chez Moi*'.**

BY ROGER MCCARTNEY 83

MEN ARE FROM MARS
I'M FROM TOTTENHAM

Secret #15: Spurs Man is Gawd's Gift to Romance. At the Start.

You must agree that at the start of a relationship, Spurs men are Gawd's gift to romance. We will organise the *Ruby*, buy some flowers from the Tesco Express on the Tottenham High *Frog,* and trawl round the gift stalls up the market for a nice bit of *tom*. Maybe even a nice new *kettle;* if she wears one.

Even when we're *brassic*, we will do this. Just as any bog standard lovesick North London fool would. Whilst I am skulking around, looking in the cupboard for me *whistle*, she will do what she does best: transform into the visual equivalent of a million dollars, by tarting herself right up special and doing up her *boat race.*

BY ROGER MCCARTNEY 84

MEN ARE FROM MARS
I'M FROM TOTTENHAM

At the beginning, it's all about the chase. Therefore I am romantic; I have to be. Faint heart never won fair sort. If I'm not romantic, then it's **Black cab for McCartney.** You're going home alone, fair lady-less, for a *Tommy tank* my son. Proactivity is sexual survival. If you want to procreate then you've got to be proactive. I know it's a complete nause, but that's how it is.

And so, I will initiate the courtship moves. When we slow dance, she will initiate the moving away moves. The first kiss will usually also emanate from the male side. And the first slap from the female side, if the timing of the first kiss is not spot on.

Evolution has given Spurs men the role of pursuers and Spurs women traditionally have the role of pursuees. I wouldn't mind being pursued for a change, but it's not going to happen. Not unless I join a boyband. And that may be unrealistic; bearing in mind I am no longer a boy.

BY ROGER MCCARTNEY 85

MEN ARE FROM MARS
I'M FROM TOTTENHAM

It is only when the chase is over and the prize secured, that we can slump down on the sofa and become our true romantic-dullard-selves. It's like DIY. All the skills are there, but the toolbox doesn't come out very often.

We will thereafter only rise to the romantic occasion once a year, on Valentine's Day. It is not, as you might believe, that our ardour begins to wane. It is more because our true reserved nature begins to win the battle for internal control.

When it comes to being romantic, we are Jekyll and Hide. We are capable of great love and romance, such as on Valentine's Day. But there is the other side of us, where we have been told for centuries to keep a stiff upper lip whilst conquering the globe. This is the everyday partner you see in front of you today, aka Mr Romantic Dullard. This side of us is more likely to give up a seat on a Titanic lifeboat than give up a seat on the Tube.

BY ROGER MCCARTNEY 86

MEN ARE FROM MARS
I'M FROM TOTTENHAM

It's not that we fall out of love. It's that we feel a fool, for showing love. Even when we were initiating the chase and making all the romantic overtures at the start, we didn't feel right. We felt like plonkers. Sure, we were good at it, but it didn't feel right. We Spurs men are naturally reserved. We haven't shaken the Victorian out of us yet. Give us a chance. It's only been a hundred or so years.

You see, inside every bloke there is a swashbuckling, falling-from-a-top-of-The-Shelf-to-deliver-chocolates-type-of-guy.

Conversely, inside Mr Start-of-Romance there is boring block of stone, waiting to break out and veg-out in front of *I'm a Celebrity. Get me Out of Here!* This version of male will breeze past the flowers stall at Tesco Express without giving it a moment's thought.

How do you keep the romance alive? In my experience, women are also Jekyll and Hide; not so much romantically but sexually. Mrs Hide may

BY ROGER MCCARTNEY 87

MEN ARE FROM MARS
I'M FROM TOTTENHAM

also tend to hijack the female persona once the first flush is gone.

If you can keep your sexy Dr Jekyll alive i.e. by wearing erotic underwear or something, then he is more likely to keep his romantic Dr Jekyll to the fore **and buy you flowers the next day.**

MEN ARE FROM MARS
I'M FROM TOTTENHAM

<u>Secret #16:</u> Are Spurs Men Up for It? And, I Don't Mean the Cup.

As I stand here in *The Billy Nick*, watching a re-run of replay of the 81 FA cup final - when Ricky Villa scored *that* goal - I am thinking of the question that has haunted Tottenham since the dawn of time: "Why are we here?" Simple: we are here to push on from last season. We all know that. But this question pales into insignificance when compared to "should I sleep with someone on the first date?"

Now, as Spurs fans, we have a certain morality code: that of the lesser-spotted orang-utan. Noel Coward had it right. I made him a Judge: "*I don't know what London is coming to — the higher the buildings the lower the morals.*" Spurs women also have a morality code: that of the greater-spotted orang-utan. You see, it's

BY ROGER MCCARTNEY 89

several notches higher. They own the high ground.

If you are used to using a high-morality blocker of say, factor ten, then you are going to block out the attraction rays from the opposite sex altogether. If you want an all-over appeal, keep your morality blocker low, and then some sex will creep through.

But why would you possibly want to sleep with someone on a first date? Three reasons: chemistry, opportunity and alcohol. It is like the ingredients for fire. Any one ingredient on its own = a damp squib; but put them all together and in the right quantities and lookout baby, it's 1666 all over again!

So, what to look for: Spurs men: look for a sort in the Jennifer Anniston mode, preferably wearing a replica Spurs *Dicky Dirt*. Don't worry if she doesn't look like the goddess that is Jennifer Anniston to start with, just have a few

BY ROGER MCCARTNEY 90

beers. She will slowly start to resemble Jennifer Anniston the more beers you have. Women: if he looks anything remotely like Hugo Lloris – then he's a keeper!

Scientists have come up with an equation to explain the scientific rationale of the chances of sleeping with someone, on the initial meeting. Why? Because it's fashionable, and they have time on their hands.

The equation is: Sum (Attraction + Chemistry + Opportunity + Alcohol) > Morality of participants = Sex.

If the sum of the first four mood enhancers is greater than the combined morality inhibitors of the two participants, then sex will occur. You can argue with Poch leaving Dele Alli out, but you can't argue with science.

Whether he will call you the next day or not is the next in the series of life's burning questions.

BY ROGER MCCARTNEY 91

Perhaps we need another calculation, the *Bastard Equation*, to work out if he's likely to call.

If the sex was good, he'll call. If the sex was out of this world, he'll Facebook you within five minutes. In fact, some of his friends might even Facebook you as well.

Non-returning of calls is not exclusive behaviour of the male sex, either. Many a lad rings a *Richard* the next day only to find he has been given Radio 1's flirt divert number and his soppy message, professing un-dying love, is liable to be read out live to six million people.

Of course, each person has his or her own individual score on the moral-ometer. Zero = morals of alley cat. Ten = routine use of chastity belt. My own score is round about the one/two mark, whereas, most of my dates are around nine. Memo to self: stop arranging dates with women from the Haringey knitting circle.

BY ROGER MCCARTNEY 92

MEN ARE FROM MARS
I'M FROM TOTTENHAM

The chances of making it to bed with someone, first night, are ridiculously low anyway.

Here's my checklist:

1) Is there any attraction shown by her towards us other than the sort of casual interest she would have towards the Gorilla enclosure at Regents Park Zoo?
2) Has she bought your "I have a PhD in nuclear physics, which I studied in between sessions at the gym" line?
3) Did she laugh when she asked you if you had a police record and you replied "Yes, "Message in a Bottle"
4) You ask her back to your place and she doesn't call Old Bill. That's a promising sign. I'm not in the mood for any agg off Plod. Again.

BY ROGER MCCARTNEY 93

MEN ARE FROM MARS
I'M FROM TOTTENHAM

5) Now she's back at your place and if you can function at all after all the alcohol you have imbibed, then you're on to a winner.
6) Wait a minute, you didn't realise there was two of them. Oh well, even better.
7) You can't function. Roll over. Go to sleep.

Of course, I'll sleep with someone on a first date. It would be rude not to. But due to the vast quantities of alcohol consumed, sleep is all I will do!

And I **will** bell her the next day, for I fall in love more often than Kerry Katona. In fact, sometimes I fall in love **_with_** Kerry Katona. But that's another story.

So, expect to hear me on radio 1, any day now.

BY ROGER MCCARTNEY 94

<u>Secret #17:</u> Fat Spurs Men Worry About Being Fat Just as Much as Fat Spurs Women.

Pat Jennings! My stomach's plans for Spurs domination must be thwarted. The BT Tower no longer dominates the skyline. My stomach does. Doing nothing is no longer an option. Besides, 'doing nothing' is so last week. It was precisely 'doing nothing' that allowed the paunch to grab a belly-hold.

Women **do not** have ownership of the weight control problem. Fat transcends the gender boundaries and men suffer the angst of weight-watching too. For women, it traditionally affects the hips, whereas in my case it is more tummy centric. My waistline is like the Tottenham High

BY ROGER MCCARTNEY 95

Road on a Saturday – it needs to be continually policed.

I look back with rose-tinted fondness to the days when old ma Dickens' little boy Charlie was just a lad with great expectations - and I didn't have to wrestle a spare tyre into my trousers each morning. The problem first arrived when I was in my middle-twenties. I woke up one day, and there the beer-belly was - like Daniel Levy - in it for the long haul. Other companions come and go, but it seems that me and my belly is one relationship that really *is* for life.

Sometimes I feel like letting the potbelly win the battle. I feel like saying to it: "Are you having a *turkish* old son? You can have the *Mickey Mouse*, the replica *Dicky*, whatever; just leave me on my *Jack Jones* bruv!"

Sure, I will slim down when there is an important project, for which it is essential to get in shape. Currently, I am engaged in the 'trying-not-to-morph-into-Johnny-Vegas' project. Also,

BY ROGER MCCARTNEY 96

whenever my flab is beginning to hamper the chances of procreation, then it is time for action on the Spurs fan's part.

So, why is the tummy an instigator of more anxiety amongst us menfolk, than going through the Congestion Zone on a weekday? Use your *loaf* bruv! It is simply because it is unattractive to the opposite sex. Der! If the beer-gut wasn't so unattractive to them *Richards* – I'd have two of them! I'll have one of them kebabs for me and one for me ol *china plate*, the belly, please.

If my figure repulses *me* – and I'm a fan of me - then what chance it will appeal to anyone with the prized double x chromosomes? I wish to attract as many women as possible, not just those that are Telly-Tubby-tolerant.

You know that saying "the past is a place I don't want to live, but it's worth visiting now and then"? Well, I wouldn't mind living there permanently, thank you very much. Especially in our double year. And I wouldn't mind seeing us

BY ROGER MCCARTNEY 97

lifting a trophy again or seeing Ricky Villa scoring *that* goal again. If there wasn't no smog and no rickets, that is. Oh, and I'll need an inside toilet, thank you very much!

I was skinny then, back in the day. Juno, I spent the first half of my life as a skinny stick insect. It was sweet mate. If girls approached at the beach, it was to kick sand in my *boat*. I was happy as, me.

Now if women approach, it is just to spend time in the shade that my bulk provides. I did experience a brief window of appearance-acceptability – a couple of distress-free months during the transition from skinny to fat....and then on with the headlong slide into obesity.

Funny how priorities change! When asked at school, what I wanted to be, who could have foretold that a more realistic lifegoal, rather than be centre forward for the Spurs, would be to walk from the Park Lane End to the Paxton Road End, without getting out of breath.

BY ROGER MCCARTNEY 98

MEN ARE FROM MARS
I'M FROM TOTTENHAM

How dare they build in a mechanism such as getting fat, to stop us gorging our boat races off? So unfair!

I am in self-imposed exile from Waitrose as the vast selection of cream cakes is simply too alluring. By 2000, my life had spiralled out of control and I was on a 200 grams of chocolate a day habit. I wasn't supplying, you understand. it was for personal use only.

So I knocked that on the head. Apart from my customary seven pints a night, I have retained only one other pig out behaviour: The Sunday Roast. I devour it with haste, and then I can spend the whole of the following week repenting at leisure.

Another tactic is the wearing of extra, extra-large shirts. I figure that no one will realise I'm overweight if I disguise myself as a dart player. Or like one of them marquees at Finsbury Park when the fair comes.

BY ROGER MCCARTNEY 99

MEN ARE FROM MARS
I'M FROM TOTTENHAM

I could try the heartbreak diet. Again. The only thing is, I'm out of the loop. So, I would need to find a sort, fall in love, behave badly for three years, get dumped, before the diet could truly kick in.

But don't worry. I'm pleased to announce the onslaught of plumpness is under control. **My waist is diminishing and my moobs are down to an C cup.**

Nuff said, yeah?

Secret #18: Two Indisputable Facts: North London is White. And Spurs Men are Commitaphobe.

A person that is tired of Tottenham Hotspurs is not necessarily tired of Life. More likely, he is tired of not having a parking space.

I'll tell you another thing I'm tired of though: those moments. Like when you walk in a room like a right plank and lose the plot as to why you're there, nah wot I mean?

It happened to me the other night. The cat was fetched in. Security bolts were on. Milk was out for the hedgehogs. Numpties on the internet

had all been insulted. But then, I forgot what comes next.

I lose sight of the bigger picture plot as well sometimes. I know there is something I've forgotten to do. Then I remember: "Oh, yes. Get married and have mini-Spurs-fans.

It dawned on me recently that the purpose of life is *not* to have a good time; It is to procreate and pass on those fiddly little things, genes. And my genes are the Spurs.

It was last week, as my forty-second birthday bore down on me, that the penny finally dropped. Duh. Hello! Earth calling Roger!

In the past, birthdays resulted in boozy celebrations up West and knees up with **Muvver Brown.** Now, I am more likely to embark on a session of binge thinking, about where it all went wrong in life. How did Mr Eligible morph into Johnny no-kids?

BY ROGER MCCARTNEY 102

MEN ARE FROM MARS
I'M FROM TOTTENHAM

I never wanted junior Lea-side-citizens – till now. Now that my fathering equipment is a bit battered and probably doesn't work anymore. I've always had a *chaplinesque* approach to fatherhood and had back-burnered the whole idea until later in life.

Now I feel like shouting to the world, "Give me a *dustbin lid*. Oh, and a *Richard* too. And see what you can do about the M25, will you?" Maybe I can't do much about the capital's transport system, but I would love to see a little **Roger or Rogella** running about before I'm *brown bread*.

For years I shunned commitment. I blanked it. I mugged it off. Now, I want to reverse-engineer it into to my life. I feel like saying "awight commitment? Come in and have a cup of *Rosy Lea* and sit in my favourite chair by the fire and watch *Match of the Day* with me. Spurs are on first. And bring all your child rearing possibilities with you mate! Sweet!"

Failure to commit is not always voluntary. A lot of it is 'wrong place, wrong time' syndrome. I cannot even blame it on my own Holloway childhood. Yes, it was grim. Move on. Charlie George did.

I never found *The One*. It is difficult enough to find *one* at all, let alone *one* with special qualities that would necessitate calling her *The One*.

I thought I had found *The One*. *The One* from Barnet. She looked like the blonde in Abba and had roughly the same impact on me as the blonde in Abba had on the rest of the World. She was a Westminster Abbey in my life: a massive monument and somewhere to go and worship. I was ready to kiss her *Aris* and eat the box it came in.

It was not so much a match made in heaven as a match made in the *Beehive* on the Seven

MEN ARE FROM MARS
I'M FROM TOTTENHAM

Sisters. Our souls would be interlocked forever. And they were too. Well, for ten months of forever anyway. I was happy as a pig in *tom*. Unfortunately, she wasn't. She had mood swings. She went up and down more times than Tower Bridge. I wasn't *The One* for her, but some pasty-faced *Berk* from Stoke Newington was. He was soft as *Jedi Knight* and twice as smelly.

Further auditions for *Wife Idol* were held but all *froggans* leading to marriage turned out to be cul-de-sacs; where you have to do one of those awkward ten-point turns to get out. You go all the way down there for naff all.

That put the mockers on that. I was like Wenger in the window, I just couldn't clinch the deal. I was far too immature – I had only just learnt to tie my *red white and blues* - whilst under the influence – and so I partied like it was 1971 again, when we won our first double.

MEN ARE FROM MARS

MEN ARE FROM MARS
I'M FROM TOTTENHAM

1999 came. Prince Died. Party over. Black cab for McCartney. All the guests had gone home or got married. Just as I was envisaging a *Last of the Summer Wine* future with my two best *chinas* – they got married. No, not to each other!

I was always the best man and never the groom. One day, Forty came up and gave me a tug. I tried to mug it off with "oi, Forty. Can I not cadge another twenty years of prime time"; but Forty went all *mutton*.

Meanwhile, Big Ben is still ticking, even If it's no longer boinging - due to renovations. Sitting on the shelf is no longer an option. I am still looking for *The One*. The nearest I've got so far to *The One* is the giant *The One Show* logo outside the BBC studios. But there is still time. Time is what we *do* have. A willing baby-machine is what we *don't* have. But I'm working on it. I went into *Babies R Us* to buy a baby the other day. They looked at me as if I was from Spurs. I didn't

 BY ROGER MCCARTNEY 106

react well. I threw their toys out of one of their prams.

I might not have had children yet, but I'm not going to give up practising. For just like Spurs, when you're tired of practising for a baby, you're tired of life. And, If I ever even think of giving up finding a nice little *trouble and strife* for yours truly, no doubt the Bow bells will chime to me "Turn again, Roger Mac".

So, what are the chances of me muvver becoming me grand-muvver any time soon? As a great man and famous – not from Spurs - used to say, "*Not a Lot*".

In the words of a famous non-Spurs fan, Johnny Lydon: **"No Future!"** but there is always a future when you follow the Spurs. We are the top team in North London.

And when it comes to having a child, I am given hope from the words of an even more famous

MEN ARE FROM MARS
I'M FROM TOTTENHAM

Spurs man, Mick Jagger: *"If you start me up, I'll never stop"*.

Printed in Great Britain
by Amazon